MAY 09 2009

DATE			

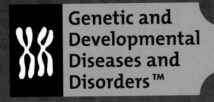

Genetic and Developmental Diseases and Disorders™

Autism

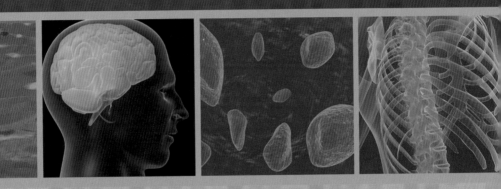

Jeri Freedman

ROSEN
PUBLISHING®

New York

Published in 2009 by The Rosen Publishing Group, Inc.
29 East 21st Street, New York, NY 10010
www.rosenpublishing.com

Library of Congress Cataloging-in-Publication Data

Freedman, Jeri.
Autism / Jeri Freedman. — 1st ed.
    p.cm.—(Genetic and developmental diseases and disorders)
Includes bibliographical references and index.
ISBN-13: 978-1-4042-1852-9 (library binding)
1. Autism. I. Title.
RC553.A88F74 2009
616.85'882—dc22

                                                            2007040006

Manufactured in Malaysia

On the cover: Background: network of human brain neurons.
Foreground: computer-generated image of the human brain.

Contents

Introduction

Autism is a disorder that affects the development of the brain. Symptoms of the disorder appear when a child is very young. Most types of autism affect boys much more frequently than girls. Autism is usually diagnosed by the time a child is three years old. Sometimes it can be identified in children who are as young as eighteen months old. This is the youngest age at which definite signs of autism may be picked up by parents or doctors.

Autism affects all aspects of a person's development. Autism affects about three to five of every one thousand children. This rate has been rising in the last few decades. We will look at some possible reasons for this increase in chapter three.

People with autism have problems talking and understanding, and they usually have poor social skills. They frequently have difficulty learning to speak, and they don't use language the way that would be expected at a given age. People with autism often play by themselves

Here, an autistic child plays alone. Programs at special schools for severely autistic children often include training to help them learn to play with other children.

and don't seek out others to share their feelings with or talk to. They repeat movements or behaviors, such as rocking or tapping, over and over.

Children with autism often have very sensitive senses. They may experience what they see, taste, smell, hear, or touch more strongly than normal. As a result, they may be made nervous by bright lights, loud noises, smells, tastes, and being touched. They may appear withdrawn and avoid contact with other people.

The Autism Spectrum Disorders

The most severe form of autism is usually just referred to as "autism." However, there is a range of other, similar problems, from not so bad to very severe. These are all called autism spectrum disorders (ASDs), and they have varying degrees of symptoms. The autism spectrum disorders include Asperger syndrome, Rett syndrome, and childhood disintegrative disorder (CDD). Asperger syndrome is a mild form of autism. People with this disorder usually have normal intelligence but are obsessive about their own interests. It is hard for them to see things from other people's points of view and to sense what others are feeling. In addition, they may be unusually sensitive to what they see, hear, taste, feel, and touch. Rett syndrome and childhood disintegrative disorder are rare. One of the most noticeable symptoms is that a child loses communication and social skills she or he previously had. Rett affects girls almost exclusively and affects one child in ten thousand to fifteen thousand. CDD affects mostly boys, but only about one in fifty thousand. Finally, there is a disorder called pervasive development disorder (PDD) not otherwise specified. This includes any disorder that has autism-like symptoms that doesn't clearly fall into one of the other categories.

What Causes Autism?

Scientists have determined that there is a genetic aspect to autism. As discussed in this book, recent research has shed light on some defective genes that can lead to autism. There is strong evidence that autism can be hereditary, meaning it is linked to genes that are passed from parents to their children. However, other factors may also contribute to autism. These include immune system problems and exposure to toxic (poisonous) substances.

What Autism Isn't

Autism is not a mental illness. The roots of autism are in the brain itself, not necessarily in the mind. Autism isn't mental retardation. People with autism have normal memories. Some children with autism have below-normal intelligence; many have normal levels of intelligence. However, children with autism may give the impression of not being as smart as other children because of their problems with talking or because they appear awkward in social situations. In many cases, those with autism spectrum disorders are actually as smart as other people. Those with Asperger syndrome sometimes are very smart.

This book starts with a history of autism. It then looks at how autism and genetics may be related, as well as how autism is diagnosed and treated. Finally, it discusses the current research in the field and how new gene-based therapies may someday be used to treat this disorder.

The History of Autism

The word "autism" was coined in 1911 by Eugen Bleuler, a Swiss doctor. He based the term on the Greek word *autos*, which means "self." He used the term to describe patients who withdrew into their fantasies. However, the disorder he was actually treating was the one we now call schizophrenia. This is a disorder in which patients suffer from hallucinations and other mental problems. The actual disorder of autism was not identified until 1943, when Dr. Leo Kanner identified it in children he studied at Johns Hopkins Hospital in Baltimore, Maryland. The children had a noticeable lack of interest in other people and repeated the same behaviors over and over.

In 1944, Dr. Hans Asperger, a German scientist, identified a milder form of the disorder

People with Asperger syndrome sometimes have exceptional skills. This boy with Asperger syndrome has highly developed artistic talent for someone his age.

that featured problems in communication and social interaction. However, Asperger patients were able to function rather well, despite their problems in certain areas. This form of autism is referred to as Asperger syndrome.

Refrigerator Moms

Kanner's term "autism" was already associated with the known mental disorder schizophrenia. This led early researchers to believe that the disorder had a mental, rather than biological, cause. Kanner believed that both mental and biological elements played a role in autism. Not all experts agreed with him, however. One influential expert in childhood disorders was Bruno Bettelheim. Bettelheim was director of the University of Chicago's Sonia Shankman Orthogenic School, which treated children with mental disorders. Bettelheim believed that autism was a mental disorder caused by "refrigerator mothers." He used this term to describe mothers who he claimed were cold to and distant from their children. From the 1940s to the 1960s, it was common to blame the mother if a child was autistic. Then, in 1990, Bettelheim was discredited when people discovered that he had lied about his academic training and made up many of his reports. Unfortunately, Bettelheim's theory had already become popular, and most doctors considered autism to be a mental problem rather than a developmental disorder. Thus there was a need for better research about the cause of autism and a need for better treatments.

Discovering the True Nature of Autism

By the 1960s, autism was identified as its own disorder, one that was different from both schizophrenia and mental retardation. Psychologist Bernard Rimland was a key figure in changing the way experts viewed autism. In 1964, Rimland wrote a book called *Infantile Autism: The Syndrome and Its Implications for a Neural Theory of Behavior*. The book discussed the possible genetic basis of autism. In 1967, Rimland founded the Autism Research Institute.

In 1965, Dr. O. Ivar Lovaas and colleagues at the University of California–Los Angeles developed a treatment for autism called applied behavior analysis (ABA). They attempted to change the behavior of autistic children by rewarding them when they behaved in a desired way. The modern version of this treatment is described in chapter three.

Dr. Bernard Rimland (above) became interested in autism in
the late 1950s, when he diagnosed his son with the disorder.
Dr. Rimland died in November 2006, at the age of seventy-eight.

In 1967, the International Classification of Diseases and Related Health Disorders recognized "infantile autism" as a disorder but still considered it a form of schizophrenia. Doctors' views of the disorder were changing, however. By the 1970s, studies comparing parents of autistic and normal children revealed that there were no differences in the parents' personalities. Since the parents of both normal and autistic children treated them the same way, it was clear that parents' behavior alone didn't cause autism. The fact that autism had a biological or genetic basis was becoming more obvious.

Finally, in 1977, Dr. Susan Folstein of Tufts University in Massachusetts led a study of the chromosomes of identical twins that demonstrated a definite genetic link to autism. Chromosomes are the structures in our cells that carry our genetic blueprint. They are made up of genes, which are short sequences of DNA (deoxyribonucleic acid). Each gene carries the code for one protein—a substance that affects a body function or makes up a type of tissue in the body. Folstein's study identified sites on chromosomes 7 and 13 as possibly being involved in autism.

Advances in Diagnosis and Treatment

The *Diagnostic and Statistical Manual* is the guide the American Psychiatric Association uses to diagnose and characterize mental illnesses. In 1980, the authoritative manual recognized autism for the first time as a developmental disorder with a probable biological basis. In 1989, Drs. Catherine Lord, Michael Rutter, and Ann Le Couteur developed the Autism Diagnostic Interview, a tool that can be used to diagnose people suspected of having autism. In 1990, Drs. Stanley Greenspan and Serena Wieder developed a new treatment for autism, called Floortime. Floortime is based on new brain research that

This photo illustrates some of the methods used in Floortime. Here, a special teacher tries to get a boy with autism to focus on her and include her in his play.

shows that human development is based on interactions with other people. In contrast to ABA, which tries to change behavior, Floortime focuses on improving social skills, imagination, and emotional abilities. Once it was known that autism has a primarily biological basis, the focus in the 1990s and 2000s switched to finding the biological and genetic causes of autism.

Famous People with Autism

Many people with autism spectrum disorders have gone on to have successful careers. Among these are actress Daryl Hannah (from the *Kill Bill* movies); American poet Christopher Knowles;

His extreme shyness, inability to make eye contact, nervous tics, and use of repeated patterns in his art have led experts to suspect that artist Andy Warhol had autism.

Satoshi Tajiri, creator of *Pocket Monsters* and *Pokemon*; and Raymond Thompson, creator of the teen television series *The Tribe*.

In addition, experts have examined the behavior of a number of people who lived before autism was a known disorder. Researchers suspect that the following people may have suffered from autism spectrum disorders:

- **Albert Einstein** (1879–1955), scientist who developed major theories of modern physics, including the theory of relativity, and winner of the Nobel Prize for Physics
- **Andy Warhol** (1928–1987), American artist and key figure in the pop art movement
- **Nikola Tesla** (1856–1943), Hungarian scientist and inventor who pioneered many of the electrical devices that form the basis of modern electronics
- **William Butler Yeats** (1865–1939), Irish poet and playwright, and winner of the Nobel Prize for Literature

Genetics and Autism

2

Genetic information is carried by chromosomes, threadlike elements found in the nucleus (center) of cells. Chromosomes are made of the chemical compound deoxyribonucleic acid (DNA). Chromosomes are made up of genes, each one a unique sequence of DNA. A gene or combination of genes carries the code for a specific trait, such as hair color or eye color. Most genes can be found at a specific place on a specific chromosome. This helps researchers identify which gene is responsible for a given trait.

Every cell in the body except for sperm and egg cells contains twenty-three pairs of chromosomes. Sperm and egg cells contain only one-half of each pair of chromosomes. That way, sperm and egg cells combine to create a

TCGATTCTCAACATGATACGTACTCGTCCACTACAACTGAACTCGAGAGGTACTA

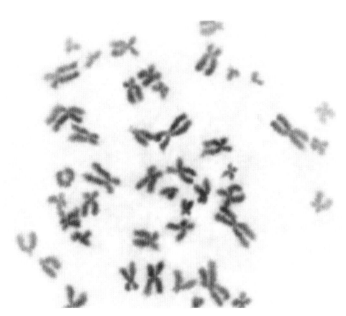

These are human male chromosomes. Scientists apply a dark dye to the chromosomes so that they are easier to study and photograph.

baby with a complete set of twenty-three pairs of chromosomes. You get one of each type of chromosome from your mother and one from your father.

The Genetic Basis of Autism

Each gene carries the code for a cell to produce a certain type of protein—one of the basic building blocks of the body. Sometimes, a gene gets damaged or undergoes a change called a mutation. This change can cause the gene to function incorrectly, or even not at all. When this happens, the protein that the gene makes is not produced or is made incorrectly.

When the human body relies on these defective genes to function, it can lead to problems such as autism.

Defects in genes can occur in three ways:

- A defective gene can be passed from a parent to a child in the chromosomes.
- A gene may be damaged by exposure to a virus or toxic substance in the environment.
- A gene may mutate accidentally when embryo cells duplicate.

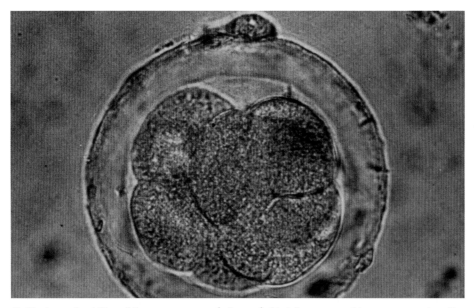

Cells in a fertilized human egg *(above)* divide many times, eventually forming an embryo. Occasionally, a mistake occurs when the genes in the cell are copied.

Autism is not a single disorder. It is a group of disorders with similar symptoms. Since autism occurs in a variety of ways and to different degrees, it cannot be just a problem with a single gene. According to the U.S. National Institutes of Health (NIH), recent research shows that there may be twelve or more different genes that play a role in autism. Problems with these genes can have three different effects:

- They can make a person more likely to develop autism. This is called susceptibility.
- They can cause a particular symptom to occur.
- They can make a symptom worse.

How Do We Know Autism Is Genetic?

The first thing that researchers have had to find out is whether or not autism is a genetic disorder. A family study is one of the best ways to find out. Families with twins are particularly useful when it comes to studying autism and other genetic disorders. Fraternal (nonidentical) twins have the same parents, but the genetic material they inherited from them is combined in different ways. These twins are as genetically similar as other brothers or sisters. The genetic makeup of identical twins, on the other hand, is exactly the same.

Scientists have found that when one fraternal twin has autism, the other twin also has autism less than 7 percent of the time. However, when one identical twin has autism, more than 60 percent of the time the other twin also has the disorder. This is strong evidence that there is a genetic aspect to autism.

Researchers have also studied non-twin brothers and sisters of people with autism, finding that 2 to 8 percent of the time the non-twin siblings have autism, too. This percentage of autism is similar to that of fraternal twins.

These identical twins both have autism. When people with the same genetic makeup have the same symptoms, there is often a genetic basis to the problem.

Finding the Autism Gene

Finding out that autism is genetic is just the beginning. Researchers must locate the genes responsible for the disorder. There are several different ways to do this. One approach is to find out what is different about genes in particular locations. For this, scientists perform cytogenetic studies. ("Cyto" means "cell.") They take some cells from a person who has autism and stain the chromosomes from those cells with a dye. This makes various regions of the chromosome appear as light and dark bands. Researchers then examine the chromosomes under a microscope and compare them to those of a person who does not have autism. Regions where the light and dark bands

MERCURY AND VACCINES

In the past, some people suspected that autism could be caused by exposure to vaccines given to children to protect them from childhood diseases. This is now known not to be true and has been proven by many research studies. It was previously thought that the MMR (measles/mumps/rubella) vaccine could trigger the immune system to attack the body's own nerve cells. Other people believed that the culprit was a mercury-containing chemical added to vaccines to keep them from spoiling. It is known that eating a lot of mercury can cause brain and nerve problems. However, blood tests of autistic children have failed to show a greater level of mercury than in other children.

These theories rest on the coincidence that children receive their first MMR vaccine around fifteen or eighteen months of age, which is the same time that autism symptoms may first appear. However, the fact that two things happen at the same time does not mean that one caused the other. Several recent studies of vaccines have found no link between vaccines and autism. Indeed, the number of children being given vaccines has remained stable, while the number of children being diagnosed with autism has continued to rise.

look different may indicate the locations of genes that are responsible for autism. Researchers can then investigate the genes in those regions of the chromosomes.

Gene sequencing is one of the ways in which researchers investigate the genes in question. Genes are made up of combinations of four basic elements called bases. In human beings, these bases are nucleotide chemicals called adenine, guanine, cytosine, and thymine. These bases combine in sequences to

A scientist uses a microscope to examine a cell that has been stained with a dye, letting her clearly see the structures inside the cell.

form the structure of DNA. In gene sequencing, researchers use chemicals and heat to make copies of segments of a person's DNA. They can "tag" each different type of base with a marker, such as a uniquely colored dye. This allows them to examine the DNA and see exactly which bases are where. Sometimes the bases are not in the place they normally occur. Other times, particular bases are in certain locations known to represent a mutated form of a gene. In both of these cases, researchers can recognize that the gene has a mutation.

Sometimes researchers sequence the genome (all the genetic material) of a family that has a member with autism. They then examine the results to see how the genome of the autistic person is different from the genome of people without autism. They pay particular attention to areas of chromosomes that other studies suggest may be linked to autism. Throughout the late twentieth and early twenty-first centuries, scientists have learned about the specific functions of many genes. This knowledge allows researchers to look at specific genes and groups of genes that control the functions that are affected by autism. Comparing these genes in people with and without autism allows researchers to identify differences that might lead to the disorder.

Sometimes, researchers work in the opposite direction— from treatment to cause. They do this by seeing which medications improve the symptoms of the disorder. Next, they figure out which processes in the body are affected by the medication. Then, they examine the genes that play a role in controlling those processes. If one or more of those genes is changed or missing in a person with autism, then the gene in question may be significant in autism.

Which Genes Cause Autism?

Research has provided evidence of the factors that contribute to autism. These include genetic factors, imbalances in chemicals that control brain processes, exposure of the fetus to toxic substances while in the womb, and immune system problems.

From the genome screening studies, scientists have found parts of several different chromosomes that appear to play a role in autism. Problems have been found on specific areas of chromosomes 2, 7, 13, 16, 17, and the X chromosome. Chromosome 2, for example, contains thirty-eight genes responsible for early growth and development. These genes are called homeobox, or HOX, genes. These are very important for the proper development of the cerebellum (the back part of the brain that controls coordination) and the brain stem (the bottom of the brain connecting to the spinal cord that controls reflexes and breathing). These parts of the brain are affected in people with autism. One area of chromosome 7 has been labeled AUTS1 because it contains genes responsible for language processing and speech that are involved in autism.

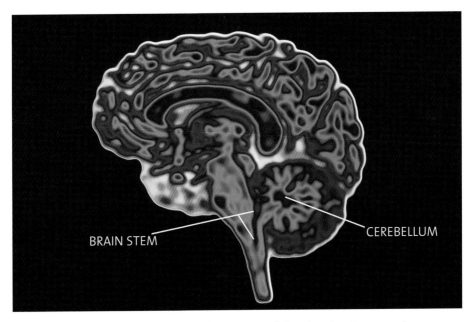

BRAIN STEM

CEREBELLUM

This is a computer-generated image of the brain. Researchers strongly suspect the cerebellum and brain stem each play important roles in autism.

These other types of genes also contribute to autism:

- Genes responsible for controlling the growth of nerve cell connections.
- Genes that affect the functioning of the neurotransmitter (a chemical that affects brain and nerve function) serotonin.
- Genes that affect immune system function. The immune system protects the body against foreign invaders such as bacteria. If the immune system malfunctions, it can wrongly attack the body itself.

The Human Side of Autism

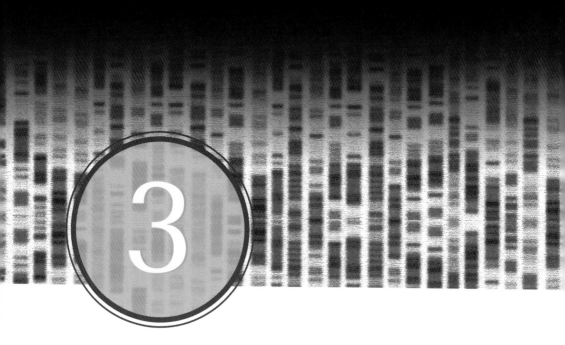

This chapter explores some of the major issues relating to identifying, treating, and living with autism.

Symptoms of Autism

The diagnosis of autism begins with observation. Parents, preschool/kindergarten teachers, doctors, and day care workers all have the opportunity to observe children.

Children with autism may have noticeable problems in communication and social skills. The following is a list of some common symptoms that one might see in a child with autism. It is important to remember that many children will normally exhibit these symptoms, at least some of the time:

- As a baby, doesn't babble or point to people or objects
- Does not speak words or combinations of words appropriate for his or her age
- Doesn't respond to smiling or frowning
- Avoids looking people in the eye
- Prefers being alone to playing with others
- Engages in repetitive behavior such as rocking, or repeatedly lines up toys or objects
- Resists being cuddled or touched
- Shows extreme sensitivity to sounds, tastes, light, or touch
- Becomes violent or aggressive when frustrated

In addition to observable symptoms, children with autism sometimes suffer from physical problems. A small percentage

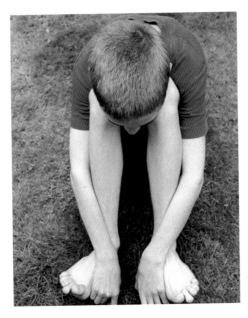

Children with autism are often withdrawn and do not interact normally with the environment. Extremely sensitive senses may be one reason for this behavior.

of people with autism have very serious physical problems that can shorten their lifespan. However, most people with autism live about as long as other people. About 25 percent of those with autism experience seizures, or bursts of abnormal electrical activity in the brain. Seizures can cause uncontrollable muscle movements, staring into space, or other strange movements. Also, about 1 to 4 percent of those with autism also have tuberous sclerosis, a genetic disease that causes small tumors to form in the brain and other organs. People can also have tuberous sclerosis without having autism, though.

Screening for Autism

Several different screening tests have been created to test whether children are developing the social and communication skills they should have for their age. These include the Checklist of Autism in Toddlers (CHAT), the modified Checklist for Autism in Toddlers (M-CHAT), the Screening Tool for Autism in Two-Year-Olds (STAT), and the Social Communication Questionnaire (SCQ). In some cases, a doctor or other health professional asks parents a series of questions. Other tests rely on a combination of parental responses and observation of the child. These tests are not designed to diagnose particular problems, only to pick up on cues that a child might have an autism spectrum disorder. If it seems that this might be the case, the next step is to go for further testing by professionals who deal with autistic children.

Some children have "high-functioning" autism, meaning that they behave normally in many ways and are not debilitated by their condition. Children with high-functioning autism and Asperger syndrome may not show developmental problems or have difficulties in using language. As a result, they are often not identified by the standard screening tests. Therefore, special

A doctor talks with a child during a medical visit. Observing children in such situations is one way doctors check a child's social development.

tests have been created to identify individuals who might have these disorders. These tests include the Autism Spectrum Screening Questionnaire, the Australian Scale for Asperger Syndrome, and the Childhood Asperger Syndrome Test. For the Asperger tests, screeners usually ask parents questions that focus on the social behavior of their child instead of language problems.

Diagnostic Testing

If a routine screening test indicates that a child might have an autism spectrum disorder, the next step is an evaluation by a team of specialists. This may include a neurologist (brain doctor), a psychologist, a speech therapist, a neurodevelopmental pediatrician, and/or other experts in particular developmental areas. The child's thinking and language skills are tested. The evaluation may involve doing a scan of the child's brain, such as a magnetic resonance imaging (MRI) scan. MRI is a technique that uses large magnets to create a picture of the child's brain. Using this image, doctors can see if there are any brain defects that might account for any problems revealed in the screening

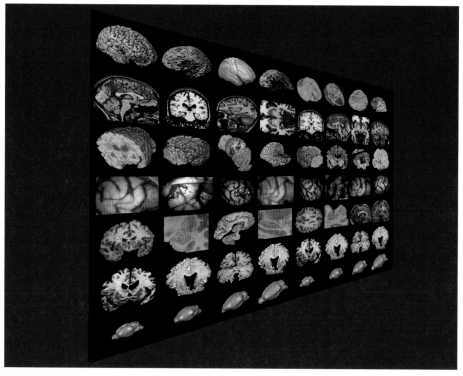

These pictures are produced by various imaging techniques used to look at the brain. The images help doctors find defects or tumors that could cause symptoms of disease.

tests. A DNA analysis may also be done to look for known genetic mutations. However, this approach will likely be more useful in the future, as scientists learn more about which mutations are responsible for autism.

The child will also be given a hearing test and a test for lead poisoning. Lead poisoning can lead to nerve and brain problems. Deafness can obviously lead to problems with a child's ability to speak, since the child can't hear words being spoken. These tests rule out some non-autism-related problems.

A number of other tests have been created specifically for diagnosing autism. Autism occurs in many different forms and to different degrees, and these tests help identify children with autism spectrum disorders. In addition, they provide valuable information on each child's specific problems so that experts can work with the child's parents to develop a customized treatment plan.

The Autism Increase Controversy

In the United States, the diagnosis of autism spectrum disorders has increased over the last decade. The number of children diagnosed has increased from four to five per ten thousand in the 1980s to thirty to sixty children per ten thousand in the 1990s, according to a report in the August 2003 issue of *Journal of Autism and Developmental Disorders*. In the 2000s, experts estimate that fifty-five to sixty-five of every ten thousand babies born will have an autism spectrum disorder.

Why has the rate of autism increased so much? Some experts point to environmental factors. Others, however, suggest that the percentage of children with autism has not increased. They believe that the rate is increasing simply because more doctors are diagnosing children with autism. There are two sides to this argument.

First, until the late twentieth century, autism was not recognized as a distinct disorder. Now that it is better known, more children with autism are being identified. In the past, they might simply have been labeled "slow," "stupid," "schizophrenic," or "antisocial." In addition, this count includes those who have high-functioning autism and autism spectrum disorders such as Asperger syndrome. These children would likely not have been diagnosed as autistic in the past because they were able to function in society.

Second, it is possible that children who exhibit some of the signs of autism are mistakenly being diagnosed as autistic. For example, doctors may misdiagnose children who show a lack of empathy for their peers, have a tendency to act up in class, or are shy and don't talk much. Some people even question whether Asperger syndrome is actually a form of autism. They suggest that there isn't only one way that people should behave socially and that it is normal to want to spend time alone rather than with other people. They believe that there is a broad range of behavior that is normal for people and that it may include behaviors that others label as autistic. In addition, many very bright children are bored by the activities of their peers. They may prefer to spend time alone reading or exploring areas that interest them. Or they may avoid others because their peers pick on them for being different.

Treatment for Autism

Since autism is a genetic disorder that cannot be reversed or "cured," medical treatments for autism are aimed at reducing the symptoms. Severe medical symptoms, such as seizures and compulsive behavior (performing the same behavior over and over), are frequently treated with medications. Children with autism often have trouble controlling their emotions and may be prone to aggressive or violent outbursts when frustrated. Medications have been shown to help control such behavioral problems in autistic children. Most of these drugs block the activity of dopamine, another neurotransmitter (chemical) in the brain.

Some people have suggested that food allergies or the lack of a certain vitamin or mineral can lead to autism. However, thus far, studies have not shown any conclusive evidence that this is the case.

Behavioral Training

Currently, there is no cure for autism. It is also not possible to make all the symptoms go away by taking medication. Much of the treatment is currently aimed at improving the behavior of those with the disorder so that they can interact with the world and other people in a more functional way.

One of the most successful treatments is applied behavior analysis (ABA). A form of this technique, called early and intensive behavior intervention, has been shown to be especially useful. The goal of this approach is to discourage nonproductive behaviors that make it more difficult for the child to interact or communicate with others. At the same time, the child is encouraged to improve communication and other skills that will allow him or her to interact with other people and function at school or in public. This typically involves a trainer working intensively with a child for many hours each week. The child is taught what is expected in certain situations and then drilled in the appropriate behaviors.

When they reach school age, children with autism may attend either special schools or public schools with programs

Training can help autistic children learn to perform tasks most children do naturally. Here, a boy with autism is taught to string words together to form sentences.

for children with disabilities. They may have specially designed course loads. If they attend a school that is equipped to teach autistic children, they will also receive training in life activities such as shopping and using public transportation. As they enter their teenage years, people with autism may also need parental support or professional assistance in dealing with sexual issues and social issues, such as dating and finding a job.

Living with Autism

Eventually, children with autism grow up. They are then faced with finding a place to live and, in some cases, a job. Not all people with autism can live on their own. Some continue to live at home. Others live on their own but require regular assistance from a relative, a professional such as a social worker, or a caretaker who is hired by the family. Some people live in foster homes, which are private homes where people take care of adults with disabilities. They may also live in a group home, where people with disabilities live together, along with professionals who help them with their daily needs. While it is desirable for people to live as normal a life as possible, some people are so severely disabled that they need to live in long-term-care institutions, which provide constant help and supervision.

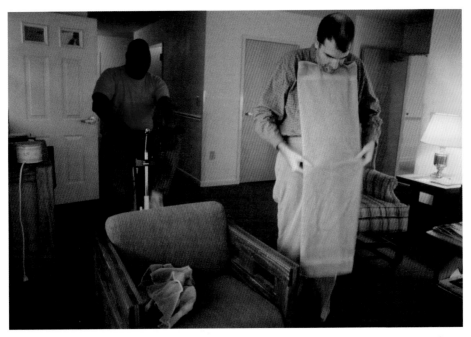

Group homes allow people with autism to socialize normally. They can engage in everyday activities, while professional assistance is available when needed.

Many with high-functioning autism can hold down regular jobs. They may have difficulties in communication and social skills but still do well at work, especially in jobs that don't involve a lot of talking or social interaction. According to a Web site called This Way of Life (http://www.thiswayoflife.com), people with autism report liking such jobs as computer programmer, truck driver, bookstore clerk, and historical researcher. Many schools for autistic children provide job training that teaches them to perform basic types of work that will allow them to earn a living. Another alternative is employment through a sheltered workshop or job program where people perform supervised work.

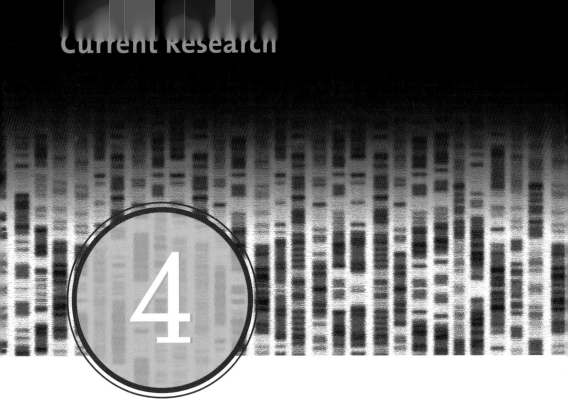

4

Scientists are performing several different types of studies to understand the genetic basis of autism. This section examines some of those studies.

 ## Brain Imaging Studies

Modern technology gives researchers a variety of machines that allow them to take pictures of living people's brains. For example, researchers often use techniques such as magnetic resonance imaging (MRI) to produce an image of the brain. In MRI, the person is placed in a machine, and large magnets are turned on, causing all the atoms of hydrogen in the body to line up the same way. Then a radio wave is bounced off them. This causes the atoms to flip and emit a signal. A computer analyzes the signal and produces a picture of the tissue. This allows researchers to see directly which areas of the brain are different in people with autism and in what ways. Several different types of brain imaging studies are currently being used to investigate autism.

Brain Size and Shape

Imaging studies have shown that the brains and heads of children with autism grow abnormally large early in life. However, the size difference seems to lessen as the child goes through late childhood and becomes a teenager.

A technique called magnetic resonance spectroscopy (MRS) helps researchers identify high concentrations of specific types of brain chemicals. This has allowed researchers to study several key substances that affect the development of nerves in our brain. They found that in the brains of young children with autism, certain substances occur at lower-than-normal levels. However, the significance of this finding is unknown and is currently being investigated.

Brain Activity Imaging

Another use of brain imaging is to observe what parts of the brain are active during certain activities, and to see how this compares to the areas that are active in people who do not have autism. This approach is called functional neuroimaging. Certain areas of the brain control specific functions, such as language, movement, and so on. Therefore, researchers can focus on specific areas of the brain to see how they behave. One approach to this is called functional MRI (fMRI). Most commonly, fMRI is being used to study what happens in the brains of autistic people during social interactions. Scientists have used this technique to study people with autism who have problems with responding to facial expressions and paying

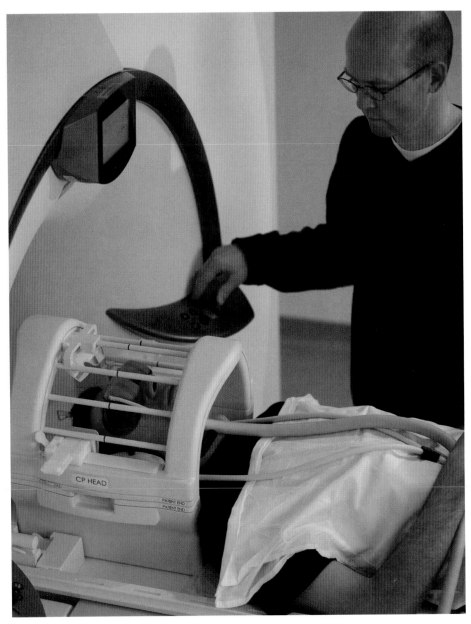

This person is being tested with an fMRI machine. The resulting images will show changes in the flow of fluids in the brain, providing information on brain function.

attention. Compared to people who do not have autism, these people have less activity in the part of the brain that recognizes motion. Also, those who have problems with social interaction and emotional response show less activity than normal in the amygdala, a part of the brain related to memory and emotion.

Identifying which parts of the brain are involved in autistic behavior provides a map for genetic research. Specific genes control the proteins responsible for the development of particular parts of the brain. Specific genes also control the chemicals that the body must produce in order for those parts of the brain to develop and function normally. It is hoped that brain imaging studies will provide valuable information as to which genes to look for.

Genetic Studies

As the genetic link to autism is now well established, a lot of current autism research is aimed at identifying exactly which genes are involved. Researchers at the David Geffen School of Medicine at UCLA have recently isolated the region on chromosome 17 where an autism gene appears to be located. They have established that this particular gene is a factor in autism only in boys. This could be one reason that the disorder more commonly occurs in males. The researchers are now carrying out DNA tests to identify the exact genetic mutation that is responsible.

In 2006, scientists supported by U.S. government research institutes studied DNA from more than 1,200 families that had more than one child with an autism spectrum disorder. Through this study, the researchers discovered a gene on chromosome 7 they linked to autism. They found that a defect in the gene causes less of a certain protein to be produced. This, in turn, upsets the way neurons, or nerve cells, grow in the brain.

AUTISM AND INFORMATION PROCESSING

In 2006, a study was conducted by researchers in the Collaborative Program of Excellence in Autism (CPEA), a research network funded by the National Institutes of Health. The study shed light on the strengths and weaknesses of children with autism. The study was performed by Dr. Nancy Minshew, professor of psychiatry and neurology at the University of Pittsburgh School of Medicine, and her colleagues. They administered a series of tests to fifty-six autistic children between the ages of eight and fifteen and fifty-six children who did not have the disorder. All of the autistic children had normal intelligence and could read and write.

The children with autism performed as well as or better than the nonautistic children on tests of concrete observation, such as finding small objects in a picture (like finding Waldo in the *Where's Waldo?* picture books). They also did well with tests of spelling and grammar. However, they had trouble with some other tasks. For example, they had difficulty telling the difference between the faces of similar-looking people. In addition, they had trouble understanding language that used metaphors. Metaphors describe something in terms of another thing—for example, "he has a heart of stone." Nonautistic children usually understand that the person's heart is not literally made of stone, but children with autism have more trouble grasping the concept. Idioms, too, created difficulties in understanding. An idiom is a nonliteral phrase whose meaning is understood by a particular group of people—for example, "hop to it." Dr. Minshew found that when this is said to an autistic child, he or she may literally start to hop, although most of us understand that the expression means "get going."

(continued on following page)

(continued from previous page)

The CPEA study suggests that autism is a disorder that affects how the brain processes information. This concept is supported by fMRI research performed by Dr. Minshew and colleagues on adults with autism. The imaging studies showed that there are problems in the way that nerves are connected, and these problems disrupt how different areas of the brain communicate with each other.

In 2007, a team of researchers at the University of Texas Southwestern Medical Center at Dallas announced that they had identified two brain cell proteins that play a role in autism. The proteins are called neuroligin-1 and neuroligin-2. Their job is to help strengthen and balance nerve cell connections.

One goal of genetic research is to find out why autism affects mostly boys. Recent research indicates that autism in boys involves different genes than autism in girls.

One of the proteins makes nerve cells more active, and the other makes them less active. The proteins were identified more than ten years ago, and mutations in them were linked to autism. Identifying these altered proteins will hopefully one day allow scientists and doctors to design specific autism treatments.

Immune System Research

Recent research suggests that the body's immune system may contribute to autism. An area of particular interest is autoimmune diseases. These are diseases involving anti-bodies, which are proteins that attach to harmful particles in the blood to mark them for destruction and removal by other immune system cells. We all make normal good antibodies against various diseases (for instance, when we receive immunizations). Studies have found that some autistic children have inappropriate antibodies in their blood that attack nerve cells of their own brains and spinal cords.

In addition, in 2003, a group of researchers at the University of Oxford in England conducted a study using blood from a mother of an autistic child. They injected the woman's blood into pregnant mice and found that the baby mice showed changes in muscle coordination and exploratory behavior. There were also changes in the cerebellum seen on MRI scans. However, mice injected with blood from mothers whose children were developing normally showed no abnormal behavior or brain changes. The researchers concluded that the mother's blood contained antibodies that attached to nerve cells in the offspring's brains. These studies indicate that there may be an autoimmune aspect to autism. Other studies are ongoing to identify which antibodies are produced and why.

CGATTCTCAACATGATACGTACTGGTCCACTAGAACTGAACTCGAGAGGTACTAC

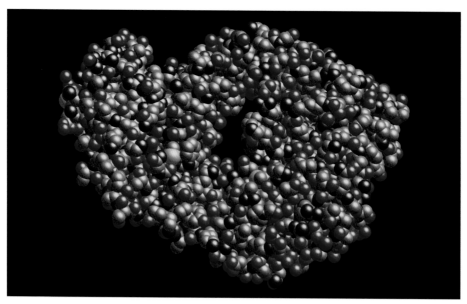

This computer model shows a molecule of a common antibody found in blood. Antibodies may play a role in autism.

Researching Treatments

Of course, the goal of autism research is to find a way to treat the disorder. One of the most exciting recent experiments occurred in 2007, at the Picower Institute for Learning and Memory at the Massachusetts Institute of Technology (MIT). Researchers there experimentally reversed mental retardation and autism-like symptoms in mice. The scientists genetically altered the mice so that they had the symptoms of a disorder called fragile X syndrome (FXS). FXS is related to a mutation in a gene on the X chromosome called FMR1. A mutation on this gene means that the activity of a certain enzyme goes on without stop. The results range from mild learning disabilities

Genetic engineering allows researchers to create mice with special characteristics. Potential treatments for disorders like autism can then be tested on the mice.

to severe autism. The mutated mice showed abnormalities similar to those in patients with FXS, including hyperactivity, purposelessness, repetitive movements, attention problems, and difficulty with learning and memory. The researchers used a chemical to inhibit the activity of the enzyme, causing the nerve cells in the brain to communicate with each other normally. The mice's behavior returned to normal, too.

The fact that the treatment worked several weeks after the mice developed symptoms of the disorder is exciting. This shows that it may be possible to develop treatments for the symptoms of autism-like disorders that are caused by genetic mutations.

5

Because of the strong genetic component of autism, it is likely that future treatment of the disorder will involve:

- Developing medications to replace missing brain chemicals caused by faulty genes, and/or
- Replacing faulty genes so that they function correctly

These approaches will require researchers to identify faulty genes, figure out which elements those genes control, and then find ways to fix the problem. This chapter examines some of the work that will probably be done in coming years to accomplish these tasks.

How Does Gene Therapy Work?

Genetic engineering (GE) is the process of fixing defects in genes that cause diseases and disorders. Gene therapy is still in the experimental stage. However, many scientists are working to find ways to fix faulty genes to treat many different diseases and disorders, including autism. In gene therapy, the first step is inserting a healthy copy of the gene into the chromosomes of the patient. This is not easy. Chromosomes are located in the center of the cell, in an area called the nucleus, which is protected by a barrier called the nuclear membrane. Genetic therapists must find a way to get the new genes across the membrane. One of most common ways to do this is to use

Genetic engineering requires high-tech equipment. This powerful microscope, for example, allows for the observation of changes that take place inside cells.

viruses. Viruses infect cells by getting across the membrane and inserting their DNA into the nucleus of a cell. This reprograms the cell to produce more of the viral DNA. For GE, scientists use particular types of viruses that have been inactivated and do not cause infection. They safely replace the virus's DNA with the good DNA they wish to get into the cell, then use the virus to deliver it to the cell's nucleus. If all goes well, the good DNA takes over the cell's defective DNA. Then, when the cell splits naturally, it will produce more cells with the good DNA, instead of the original defective DNA.

Some scientists are also looking at methods of delivering genes that don't involve viruses. Liposomes, for example, are hollow spheres made of fat that can be filled with DNA and made to pass across the cell membrane.

Before scientists can replace a defective gene, they need to know the sequence of the DNA that they want to replace. Much of the research related to autism that is planned for the near future is designed to:

- Identify the genes responsible for autism
- Identify the functions performed by the proteins the genes control

Repairing Autistic Brains with GE

How can genetically engineered genes be used to treat autism? A study by Dr. Adrian Bird offers one answer. In 2007, Dr. Bird, a molecular biologist at the University of Edinburgh in Scotland, performed revolutionary research. He repaired a form of autism, called Rett syndrome, in mice. The mice had the same genetic defect that people with the disease have, and they showed similar symptoms. Dr. Bird genetically engineered mice so that he could cause Rett syndrome by suppressing, or "turning off,"

In 2007, Dr. Adrian Bird *(left)* successfully demonstrated that it is possible to use genetic engineering techniques to treat autism-like diseases.

a gene called MECP2. Dr. Bird and his research assistant Jacky Guy also genetically engineered another gene into the mice. This second gene, when activated, could snip out the block of DNA that made the MECP2 gene produce the bad symptoms. The second gene was activated by giving the mice a drug called tamoxifen. This worked even when the mice were adults and had fully developed brains. As long as they were fed tamoxifen, the second gene snipped out the bad segment in the MECP2, reversing the symptoms of Rett syndrome.

Dr. Rudolph Jaenisch and colleagues at the Whitehead Institute produced similar results in a related study, although the mice in their study did not recover completely.

The genetic engineering techniques used by these researchers on mice do not represent a "cure" for humans with autism. However, they do show that genetic engineering techniques can be used to fix defective genes. Future research will try to figure out how genetic engineering can be applied to human beings.

New Autism Research Initiative

The National Institutes of Health recently created the Autism Centers of Excellence (ACE) program to focus on finding the causes of and treatments for autism. The program is designed to bring together teams of researchers who are experts in different areas. For example, brain imaging experts, psychologists, and geneticists may all work together. The project is set up to start with five centers in 2007, with further expansion of the program scheduled for 2008.

Research projects scheduled to begin include the following:

- Researchers at the University of Illinois–Chicago ACE center will look at genetic factors and brain functions to learn more about repetitive behaviors in people with ASD. In addition, researchers will test how genetic factors affect the way people respond to medications that could reduce these behaviors.
- Researchers at the University of California–San Diego ACE center will use brain imaging to study brain development in infants at risk for autism spectrum disorders. It is hoped that this research will help identify physical changes in the brain that might cause autism.
- Researchers at the University of Washington ACE center will try to identify genes that may lead to autism.
- Researchers at the University of Pittsburgh ACE center will develop brain-imaging techniques to study how people with autism organize and process information and experience emotion.
- Researchers at the University of California–Los Angeles ACE center will study how autism affects the ability to communicate. The researchers will examine genes, brain structure and function, and behavior, as these factors relate to communication. A special focus of this

group will be mirror neurons, brain cells that become active when someone performs an action or observes someone else performing an action.

As you can see, research into the causes of and treatment for autism is just beginning. Research into genetics and tools that have been developed in the past two decades, such as gene sequencing, have created a unique opportunity to understand this disorder.

EPIDEMIOLOGY STUDIES

Epidemiology is the study of how diseases are transmitted. Not all researchers think that the whole cause of autism lies in the genes. Several large-scale research projects are focusing on identifying environmental and biological factors that might lead to autism. The studies will follow individuals for long periods, studying changes that take place as they develop. Such projects include:

- The Childhood Autism Risks from Genetics and the Environment (CHARGE) project, funded by the National Institutes of Health, is studying one thousand to two thousand autistic children and age-matched nonautistic children. Researchers will observe and compare the effects of chemicals in food, consumer products, air pollution, and infection. The researchers are studying the children's medical records for information on possible exposures, as well as performing a variety of blood and other biological tests.
- A huge study started in 2003 is being carried out by researchers at the Mailman School of Public Health at Columbia University and the Norwegian Institute of Public Health. The plan is to gather information from 100,000

Developmental Disabilities > Research > Autism > CADDRE

CADDRE: Centers for Autism and Developmental Disabilities Research and Epidemiology

The Children's Health Act of 2000 directed CDC to establish regional centers of excellence for ASD and other developmental disabilities. These centers make up the Centers for Autism and Developmental Disabilities Research and Epidemiology (CADDRE) Network. The CADDRE Network is currently working on the Study to Explore Early Development (SEED) – a five-year, multi-site collaborative study to help identify

Topic Contents
> Autism Home
> Overview
> Symptoms
> Screening and Diagnosis
> Treatment and Therapy
> Frequently Asked Questions
> CDC Activities
> Congressional Activities
> Resources
> Partners

Quick Links

This is the welcome page of the Centers for Disease Control and Prevention's CADDRE Network Web site (http://www.cdc.gov/ncbddd/autism/caddre.htm). Visitors to the site can learn more about CADDRE and its various ongoing projects around the country.

babies in Norway and continue to follow them throughout their lives. Researchers are collecting information about exposure to environmental elements, as well as testing blood and DNA from each child and both parents to look for mutated genes.

In 2006, the U.S. Centers for Disease Control and Prevention provided $5.9 million to set up the Centers for Autism and Developmental Disabilities Research and Epidemiology (CADDRE) Network. It has funded five centers throughout the United States. Researchers will participate in a five-year study to evaluate infections, genetic factors, family history, and behaviors such as smoking. Economic factors and other influences will also be considered. What is unique about this study is that it deliberately attempts to study diverse populations in different parts of the country. It is hoped that large-scale, long-term studies like this will identify factors that lead to autism and rule out factors that do not have an effect.

Myths and Facts

Myth: Autism is rare.
Fact: In the United States today, about six children in one thousand are diagnosed with autism, making it one of the most common developmental disorders. Autism spectrum disorders affect more than one million Americans, both children and adults.

Myth: Children can outgrow autism.
Fact: Autism is a lifelong disorder. The negative effects of autism can be lessened through individual instruction and behavior therapy, and some symptoms of the disorder can be relieved using medication. However, there is no cure for autism, and children with the disorder will not outgrow it.

Myth: Autism is caused by bad parenting.
Fact: In the 1940s, influential physician Bruno Bettelheim claimed that autism was a mental disorder caused by "refrigerator moms," or mothers who were emotionally cold and distant. Today, we know autism is a developmental disorder with a biological basis and has nothing to do with bad parenting.

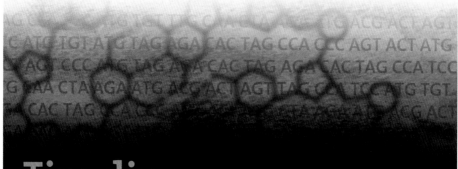

Timeline

1911

Swiss psychiatrist Eugen Bleuler coins the term "autism" to describe schizophrenia.

1943

Dr. Leo Kanner of Johns Hopkins Hospital identifies true autism in children in a paper titled "Autistic Disturbances of Affective Contact."

1944

Hans Asperger identifies a milder form of autism, later named Asperger syndrome.

1964

Bernard Rimland writes *Infantile Autism: The Syndrome and Its Implications for a Neural Theory of Behavior.*

1965

Dr. O. Ivar Lovaas develops applied behavior analysis (ABA), a treatment for autism.

1967

The International Classification of Diseases and Related Health Disorders lists "infantile autism" as a disorder for the first time; it is considered a form of schizophrenia.

Dr. Bernard Rimland establishes the Autism Research Institute.

1975

President Gerald Ford signs into law the Individuals with Disabilities Education Act. This law requires public schools to provide education to children with disabilities, including autism.

1977

Dr. Susan Folstein, a Tufts University professor of psychiatry, performs a landmark study of twins that identifies a genetic link to autism.

1980

The Diagnostic and Statistical Manual-III recognizes autism as a disorder for the first time.

1981

Dr. Lorna Wing coins the term "Asperger syndrome" in her paper about autism to describe the form of the disorder identified by Hans Asperger.

1989

Drs. Catherine Lord, Michael Rutter, and Ann Le Couteur develop the Autism Diagnostic Interview.

1990

Drs. Stanley Greenspan and Serena Wieder develop Floortime, a new form of treatment for autism.

1998

Dr. Andrew Wakefield publishes a small case study in the *Lancet*, a British medical journal, that discusses the coincident timing of MMR vaccine administration and autism diagnosis.

2004

The theory that the MMR vaccine causes autism is discredited, as multiple large studies demonstrate no causal link.

2006

Researchers supported by the National Institutes of Health isolate a gene on chromosome 7 that is clearly related to autism.

2007

Researchers at the University of Texas identify the function of two brain proteins involved in autism.

Researchers at the Massachusetts Institute of Technology succeed in reversing autism-like behaviors in mice using a chemical called p21-activated kinase.

Dr. Adrian Bird at the University of Edinburgh uses genetic engineering techniques to treat symptoms of Rett syndrome (a form of autism) in mice.

Glossary

amygdala Part of the brain involved in processing memory and emotion.

antibodies Elements of the immune system that attach to foreign invaders so that immune system cells will seek out and destroy them.

brain stem Area at the base of the brain that controls reflexes and basic body functions.

central nervous system Brain and spinal cord.

cerebellum Part of the brain that controls coordination.

chromosome Threadlike strand of DNA that carries genetic information.

cytogenetics Study of genetic material in cells.

diagnose To recognize a disease or disorder based on the observation of signs and symptoms.

empathy Ability to see or feel things from another person's point of view.

epidemiology Study of how diseases are transmitted.

gene Short sequence of DNA on a chromosome; carries the code for the production of one protein.

genetic engineering Technology used to alter the genetic material of living cells in order to make them capable of producing new substances or performing new functions.

genome Organism's complete set of DNA.

hallucination Something seen, heard, or felt that seems real but isn't actually there.

immune system Body system that protects a person against infection and toxic substances.

infantile Related to very young children.

magnetic resonance imaging (MRI) Noninvasive diagnostic procedure using a scanner to get detailed sectional images of the internal structure of the body.

mutation Change occurring to the order of bases in a cell's DNA.

neurologist Doctor who treats diseases and disorders of the brain and nerves.

neurotransmitter Chemical that allows nerve cells to communicate with one another.

nucleus Area in the center of a cell that contains chromosomes.

obsessive Persistent and irrational, as thoughts or actions.

pervasive developmental disorder (PDD) Disease that affects all parts of a person's development.

psychiatrist Medical doctor who treats diseases of the mind.

psychologist Nonmedical expert with an academic degree who treats mental and emotional problems.

schizophrenia Disorder in which patients suffer from hallucinations and other mental disturbances.

seizure Uncontrollable twitching or contracting of the muscles caused by abnormal electrical activity in the brain.

speech therapist Expert in treatment of speaking disorders.

vaccine Compound used to cause a person's immune system to form antibodies to detect and kill a specific infectious agent.

For More Information

American Psychological Association
750 First Street NE
Washington, DC 20002-4242
(202) 336-5000
Web site: http://www.apa.org/topics/topicautism.html
This organization provides information on psychological diseases; its Web site has a special section for students.

Autism Society of America
7910 Woodmont Avenue, Suite 300
Bethesda, MD 20814-3067
(301) 657-0881
Web site: http://www.autism-society.org
This organization provides information on all aspects of autism, including valuable advice on living and coping with the disorder.

National Autism Association
1330 West Schatz Lane
Nixa, MO 65714
(877) 622-2884
Web site: http://www.nationalautismassociation.org
This organization provides a variety of resources to educate and empower families affected by autism and other neurological disorders.

National Institute of Neurological Disorders and Stroke
National Institutes of Health (NIH)
9000 Rockville Pike
Bethesda, MD 20892
(301) 496-5751
Web site: http://www.ninds.nih.gov/disorders/autism/
    detail_autism.htm
One of the institutes that make up the National Institutes of Health, a part
of the U.S. Department of Health and Human Services, NINDS conducts
and supports research on brain and nervous system disorders.

Talk About Curing Autism (TACA)
P.O. Box 12409
Newport Beach, CA 92658-2409
(949) 640-4401
Web site: http://www.tacanow.com/contactus.htm
This is an organization that provides information and support to families
affected by autism.

U.S. Centers for Disease Control Autism Information Center
1600 Clifton Road
Atlanta, GA 30333
(403) 639-3534
Web site: http://www.cdc.gov/ncbddd/autism
This agency provides information on autism and resources for families.

Web Sites

Due to the changing nature of Internet links, Rosen Publishing
has developed an online list of Web sites related to the subject
of this book. This site is updated regularly. Please use this link
to access the list:

http://www.rosenlinks.com/gddd/auti

For Further Reading

Baker, Jeff. *Preparing for Life: The Complete Guide for Transitioning to Adulthood for Those with Autism and Asperger's Syndrome.* Arlington, TX: Future Horizons, 2006.

Bonnice, Sherry. *Hidden Child: Youth with Autism.* Broomall, PA: Mason Crest Publishers, 2004.

Fleischer, Leonore, Kieran McGovern, and Bob Harvey. *Rain Man.* New York, NY: Penguin, 2000.

Grandin, Temple, and Kate Duffy. *Developing Talents: Careers for Individuals with Asperger Syndrome and High-Functioning Autism.* Shawnee Mission, KS: Autism Asperger Publishing Co., 2004.

Grandin, Temple, and Sean Barron. *The Unwritten Rules of Social Relationships: Decoding Social Mysteries Through the Unique Perspectives of Autism.* Arlington, TX: Future Horizons, 2006.

Rosaler, Maxine. *Coping with Asperger Syndrome.* New York, NY: Rosen Publishing, 2004.

Rosenberg, Marsha Sarah. *Coping when a Brother or Sister Is Autistic.* New York, NY: Rosen Publishing, 2000.

Shore, Stephen, and G. Rastellis. *Understanding Autism for Dummies.* Indianapolis, IN: For Dummies/John Wiley, 2006.

Bibliography

Ashwood, Paul, Sharifia Wills, and Judy Van de Water. "The Immune Response in Autism: A New Frontier for Autism Research." *Journal of Leukocyte Biology*. May 12, 2006. Retrieved August 20, 2007 (http://www.jleukbio.org/cgi/content/full/80/1/1).

DiCicco-Bloom, Emanuel, et al. "The Developmental Neurobiology of Autism Spectrum Disorder." *Journal of Neuroscience*. June 28, 2006. Retrieved August 27, 2007 (http://www.jneurosci.org/cgi/content/full/26/26/6897).

Herbert, James D., Ian R. Sharp, and Brandon A. Gaudiano. "Separating Fact from Fiction in the Etiology and Treatment of Autism: A Scientific Review of the Evidence." *Scientific Review of Mental Health Practice*. Summer 2002. Retrieved August 20, 2007 (http://www.srmhp.org/0101/autism.html).

Jepson, Bryan, and Jane Johnson. *Changing the Course of Autism: A Scientific Approach for Parents and Physicians*. Boulder, CO: Sentient Publications, 2007.

McCoy, Krisha. "Scientists Reverse Symptoms of Autism in Mice." *HealthDay News*. June 25, 2007. Retrieved August 20, 2007 (http://www.nlm.nih.gov/medlineplus/news/fullstory_51364.html).

National Institute of Child Health and Development. "Research at the NICHD: Autism and Genes." May 2005. Retrieved August 20, 2007 (http://www.nichd.nih.gov/publications/pubs/upload/autism_genes_2005.pdf).

Notbohm, Ellen. *Ten Things Every Child with Autism Wishes You Knew*. Arlington, TX: Future Horizons, 2005.

Preidt, Robert. "Autism-Linked Proteins Help Guide Brain Cells." *HealthDay News*. June 20, 2007. Retrieved August 20, 2007 (http://www.nlm.nih.gov/medlineplus/news/fullstory_51161.html).

Science Daily Staff. "UCLA Scientists Pinpoint Region of Autism Gene on Chromosome 17." May 4, 2005. Retrieved August 20, 2007 (http://www.sciencedaily.com/releases/2005/05/050504224433.htm).

Sicile-Kira, Chantal. *Autism Spectrum Disorders*. New York, NY: HarperCollins, 2004.

Szpir, Michael. "Tracing the Origins of Autism: A Spectrum of Studies." *Environmental Health Perspectives*. July 2006. Retrieved August 27, 2007 (http://www.pubmedcentral.nih.gov/articlerender.fcgi?pubmedid=16835042).

Index

A

American Psychiatric Association, 12
amygdala, 38
antibodies, 41
applied behavior analysis (ABA),
    10, 13, 31
Asperger, Dr. Hans, 8–9
Asperger syndrome, 6, 7, 8–9,
    26–27, 30
autism
  in boys vs. girls, 4, 6, 38
  causes, 7, 9–10, 12–13, 16–17, 20,
    29–31, 40–41
  current research on, 7, 35–43
  definition of, 4, 6, 7, 18
  diagnosing, 4, 12, 24–30
  famous people with, 13–14
  future approaches to, 44–51
  and genetics, 7, 10, 12, 13, 15–23,
    30, 35, 38, 44–47, 48, 49
  "high-functioning," 26, 30, 34
  history of, 7, 8–14, 30
  increase in, 29–30
  information processing and, 39–40
  living with, 32–34

symptoms of, 4–6, 18, 24–26, 30–31
treating, 10, 12–13, 22, 30–32,
    42–43, 44
Autism Centers of Excellence
    (ACE) program, 48
Autism Diagnostic Interview, 12
Autism Research Institute, 10
autism spectrum disorders, 13, 14,
    26–28, 29, 30, 38, 48
autoimmune diseases, 41

B

Bettelheim, Bruno, 10
Bird, Dr. Adrian, 46–47
Bleuler, Eugen, 8

C

Centers for Disease Control and
    Prevention (CDC), 50
childhood disintegrative disorder
    (CDD), 6
chromosomes, defined, 15–16
Collaborative Program of
    Excellence in Autism (CPEA),
    39–40

About the Author

Jeri Freedman has a B.A. from Harvard University. For fifteen years, she worked for companies in the medical field. She is the author of more than twenty young adult nonfiction books, many published by Rosen Publishing. Among her previous titles are *The Human Population and the Nitrogen Cycle, Hemophilia, Lymphoma: Current and Emerging Trends in Detection and Treatment, How Do We Know About Genetics and Heredity*, and *Everything You Need to Know About Genetically Modified Foods.*

Photo Credits

Cover (top) © Biophoto Associates/Photo Researchers; cover (inset) © www.istockphoto.com/Sebastian Kaulitzki; cover (background left to right), p. 1 © www.istockphoto.com/Chronis Chamalidid, CDC, © www.istockphoto.com/Sebastian Kaulitzki; pp. 5, 27 © Pharnie/Photo Researchers; p. 9 © AFP/Getty Images; p. 11 Autism Research Institute; p. 13 © Ellen Senisi/The Image Works; pp. 14, 19 © Getty Images; p. 16 © Michael Abbey/Photo Researchers; p. 17 © Claude Edelman/Photo Researchers; p. 21 © Argonne National Laboratory/Science Source/Photo Researchers; p. 23 © Alfred Pasieka/Photo Researchers; pp. 25, 40 © John Birdsall/The Image Works; p. 28 © Arthur Toga/UCLA/Photo Researhers; p. 32 © Aurora/Getty Images; p. 33 © Nany J. Pierce/Photo Researchers; p. 37 © Mark Hamel/Photo Researchers; p. 42 © Alfred Pasieka/Custom Medical Stock Photo; p. 43 © Time-Life Pictures/Getty Images; p. 45 © Lawrence Migdale/Photo Researchers; p. 47 Courtesy of Dr. Adrian Bird.

Designer: Evelyn Horovicz; Editor: Christopher Roberts
Photo Researcher: Marty Levick